Boxing Legends

by Bob Italia

Published by Abdo & Daughters, 6535 Cecilia Circle, Bloomington, Minnesota 55439

Library bound edition distributed by Rockbottom Books, Pentagon Tower, P.O. Box 36036, Minneapolis, Minnesota 55435

Copyright© 1990 by Abdo Consulting Group, Inc., Pentagon Tower, P.O. Box 36036, Minneapolis, Minnesota 55435. International copyrights reserved in all countries. No part of this book may be reproduced in any form without written permission from the publisher. Printed in the United States.

Library of Congress Number: 90-083609   ISBN: 1-56239-010-4

Cover Photo by: Bettmann Archive
Inside Photos by: Bettmann Archive

Edited by Rosemary Wallner

— Contents —

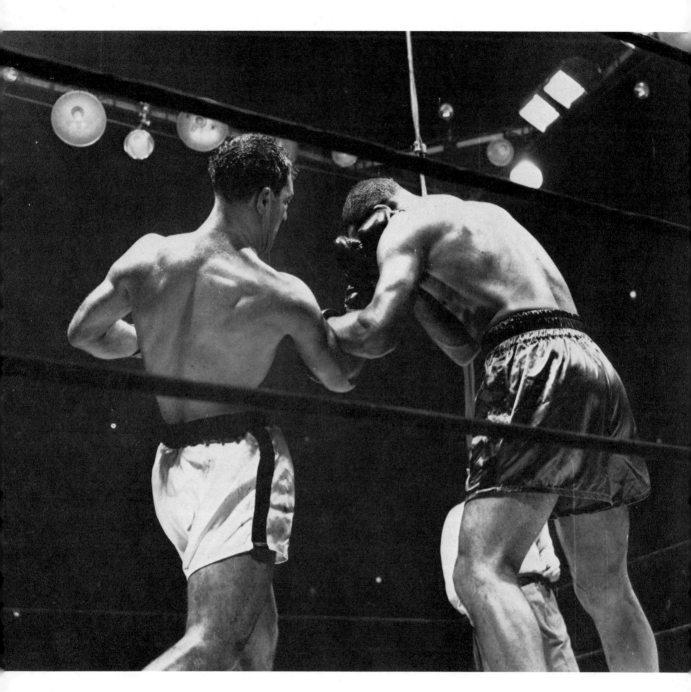

*Two boxing legends, Rocky Marciano (left)
and Joe Louis, fight it out in October 1951.*

Introduction

Boxing is the most physically punishing sport. It takes tremendous determination, stamina, strength, and courage to become a boxing champion. These five boxers have proven their greatness over the course of many years. They withstood many difficult challenges, and have earned their place in boxing history.

*Ray Junior (left) smiles along with his father,
Champion Sugar Ray Leonard.*

Sugar Ray

Ray Charles Leonard was born May 17, 1956, in Wilmington, South Carolina. Leonard was named after the famous blind singer, Ray Charles. Leonard's mother, Gertha, was a nurse. His father, Cicero, was a night clerk at a grocery store.

The Leonards never had much money, and Ray often had to wear secondhand clothing. Leonard was quiet and shy. He was a good student, and didn't get into trouble. He liked to read—especially comic books.

After the Leonards moved to Palmer Park, Maryland, Leonard often visited the Palmer Park Recreation Center. There, he got interested in boxing. Though he was small and skinny, Leonard was quick and agile. He had fast hands, and boxing came easily to him. He spent a lot of hours at the center working out and practicing his boxing in the middle of the basketball court. The center did not have a boxing ring.

In 1973, Leonard decided to enter the National Golden Gloves competition. He became the 132-pound class champion. The following year, Leonard became the American Athletic Union junior champion. And in 1975, Leonard won his class in the Pan-American competition. Leonard knew he was good enough for the upcoming Olympic games, and he began preparing hard for them.

Leonard tried out for the Olympic team and made it. He spent a month at the Olympic training camp in Burlington, Vermont, then another month training at the Olympic Village in Montreal, Canada. Leonard won the gold medal in his weight class. It was his 150th fight as an amateur. He became a favorite with the

American fans. They started calling him Sugar Ray, after the famous professional boxer, Sugar Ray Robinson.

But Leonard was not planning on a professional boxing career. He wanted to quit boxing after the Olympics. But his parents were sick and in the hospital. The medical bills were piling up. Leonard had to do something. Boxing was the only answer.

Leonard returned to Maryland and found a sponsor named Mike Trainer. He was a lawyer. Trainer collected $21,000 from other investors. Now Leonard could become a professional boxer.

Angelo Dundee, Muhammed Ali's manager, agreed to manage Leonard. On February 5, 1977, Leonard fought his first professional match against Luis "The Bull" Vega. Leonard won by decision. With his $40,000 winnings, Leonard paid his investors and his parents' hospital bills.

Leonard continued boxing—and winning. Soon he became a contender in the welterweight (147-pound) class, and was ready for a title fight.

Wilfred Benitez was the current World Boxing Council (WBC) Welterweight champion. He agreed to give Leonard a fight in Las Vegas, Nevada. ABC would televise the fight. It would be a big moment for Leonard—if he could win.

The fight started well for Leonard. He knocked Benitez down in the third round. But Benitez did not quit, and came at Leonard with a flurry of punches. The fight raged on, round after round. In the fifteenth and final round, Leonard landed a punch on Benitez's chin. The champion went down and tried to get up. But he was too dazed. The referee stopped the fight. Sugar Ray Leonard was the Welterweight champion. For his efforts, he earned $1 million. It was Leonard's twenty-sixth straight victory. He had yet to lose.

In June 1980, Leonard was still undefeated when he was challenged by Roberto Duran. Duran was a fierce fighter. He had fought in seventy-two fights with only one loss. Leonard took a severe pounding from Duran. His face was swollen and bruised. Though Leonard managed to stay with Duran for fifteen rounds the judges awarded the match to Duran. Leonard had lost his first fight— and the welterweight title.

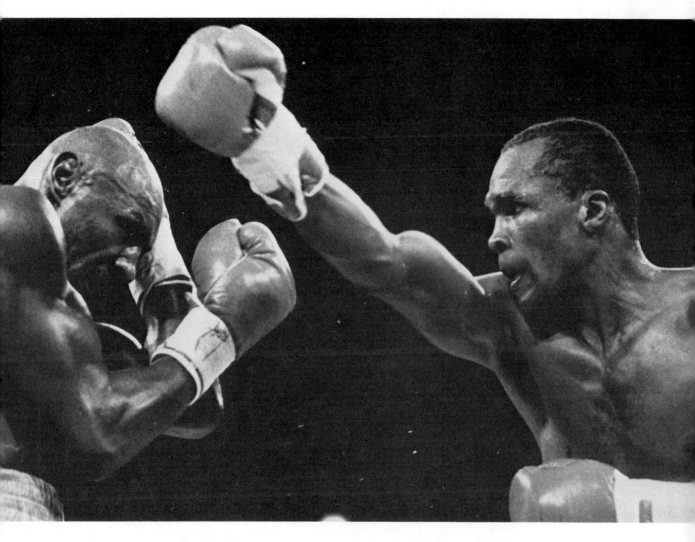

*The fight for the middleweight title against
"Marvelous" Marvin Hagler.*

Though Leonard received $8 million for the fight, he was not happy. He decided he wanted a rematch with Duran. A fight was granted for November 25, 1980. This time, Leonard kept away from Duran's deadly jabs and danced around him, hitting Duran with jabs of his own. Duran spent the entire match chasing Leonard around the ring. By the eighth round, Duran had become exhausted. Leonard moved in with a flurry of punches, and Duran cried, "No mas (No more)!" Leonard had recaptured his welterweight title.

In 1981, Leonard agreed to give Thomas "The Hit Man" Hearns a shot at the title. Hearns was the World Boxing Association (WBA) welterweight champion. If Leonard could win, he would be champion of both the WBC and the WBA.

Hearns was a tough opponent. He stood over six feet tall and had a very long reach. In the third round, Hearns landed a blow to Leonard's left eye. It swelled, and restricted Leonard's vision. The two champions battled each other round after round. But by the fourteenth round, Hearns had run out of energy. Leonard pounded Hearns on the ropes until the referee stopped the fight. Leonard was champion of both boxing organizations. But his left eye had been damaged. This injury would affect the rest of his career.

Part of Leonard's retina had come loose and gave him vision problems. Only an operation could repair the damage. Otherwise, Leonard might go blind. The operation was a success, but the doctors warned against any further boxing. Another blow to the left eye could cause permanent damage. Leonard waited for six months to decide what to do. Then he announced his retirement.

But boxing had become Leonard's life, and he wanted to return to the ring. In December 1983, Leonard announced he would resume his boxing career—as a middleweight. May 11, 1984, was Leonard's first match. He won in nine rounds over Kevin Howard. But during the fight, Leonard had been knocked down. It reminded him how dangerously close he had come to losing his sight. Afterwards, he announced his retirement again.

It would not be until April 6, 1987, when Sugar Ray Leonard returned to the boxing ring. This time, it was to fight "Marvelous" Marvin Hagler for the middleweight title. Leonard won by decision, and now had another boxing title. In November 1988, Leonard challenged light-heavyweight champion Donny Lalonde to a match—and knocked him out. Now Leonard had won titles in three different weight classes.

In June, Leonard agreed to a long-awaited rematch with Thomas Hearns at Caesar's Palace in Las Vegas, Nevada. Hearns fought with a ferociousness most thought was gone. He knocked down Leonard twice, and stayed with Leonard through the full fifteen rounds. The judges called it a draw. Leonard earned $18 million and contemplated retirement once more.

But once again, the lure of big money brought Leonard to the ring—this time, in December. The match was against the only foe who had ever beaten Leonard: thirty-eight-year-old Roberto Duran. Leonard won the fight by decision—and added $20 million to his earnings.

Having won championships in five different weight categories, Leonard has single-handedly revived interest in all boxing weight classes below the heavyweight division. With only one loss and one draw to blemish his record, Sugar Ray Leonard has established himself as one of the all-time great boxers.

*Mike Tyson (right) pummeling James "Bonecrusher"
Smith for the WBA Championship.*

Tyson

Michael (Mike) Gerard Tyson was born June 30, 1966, in Brooklyn, New York. His father, Jimmy Kirkpatrick, and his mother, Lorna Tyson, were not married. They did not even live together. Lorna Tyson lived with another man, Eddie Gillison.

Tyson's neighborhood was a slum. Everyone was poor, and few had jobs. Violence and crime were common, and accepted. When Tyson was five years old, he witnessed a murder. Tyson was so frightened, he did not leave his tiny apartment for three months.

Tyson learned early that survival in the slums depended upon fighting skills. Tyson was short, but stocky. He fought a lot with other kids in the neighborhood. By the time he was ten years old, Tyson had already obtained a bad reputation. No one dared touch him or any member of his family. He quit school and hung around with his peers on street corners. When he got bored, Tyson turned to stealing and drinking. Tyson thought drug dealers and thieves were cool.

When he was twelve years old, Tyson's life began to turn around. That's when he was sent to the Tyron Reform School in Johnstown, New York. At Tyron, Tyson discovered something that interested him, something that was better than fighting on the streets. It was boxing.

Tyson turned all his energies to the sport of boxing and stayed off the streets. In 1979, Tyson's powerful 5-foot 6-inch, 185-pound build caught the eye of boxing manager Cus D'Amato. D'Amato was convinced Tyson could be a heavyweight contender if he practiced hard and stayed out of trouble. Tyson agreed.

Tyson joined the Junior Olympics boxing program and won all his matches with ease. Then, in 1981, he won the Junior Olympic heavyweight championship. He was only fifteen years old.

Afterwards, Tyson had trouble finding opponents. When other managers discovered their fighters would be facing Tyson, they often pulled their fighters from the tournaments. It got so bad, D'Amato had to pay professional boxers just to spar (practice) with the teenage Tyson. In fifty-two amateur fights, Tyson won forty-seven. Now he was ready to become a professional boxer.

In 1985, Tyson won his first professional match. In his second fight, Tyson knocked out his opponent after fifty-two seconds of the first round. Then, in his next fight, Tyson knocked out his opponent in the fourth round. Word was spreading quickly that Tyson was a powerful and dangerous fighter. Many professional boxers withdrew from their matches with nineteen-year-old Mike Tyson.

Tyson's first big professional fight came in October 1985 in Atlantic City against twenty-seven-year-old Donnie Long. Long was considered a good fighter, and many thought he would be a tough test for Tyson. Tyson attacked Long from the opening seconds of the first round. The fight was stopped a minute later. Tyson had won.

Tyson won his next few matches with ease. Rarely did the fights go beyond four rounds. All ended in knockouts. After Tyson won his match against a tough Jesse Ferguson in 1986, many sportswriters were conceding that Mike Tyson was truly a heavyweight contender. It was time to find out for sure.

Marvis Frazier was Tyson's next big challenge. Frazier was already considered one of the rising stars in heavyweight boxing. Tyson and Frazier fought on July 26, 1986. Like he always did, Tyson went after his opponent the instant the bell rung, signalling the beginning of the match. Thirty seconds later, the referee stopped the fight. Tyson had won again by a knockout—the fastest ever in TV boxing history. Now it was time to fight for the title.

World Boxing Council (WBC) heavyweight champion Trevor Berbick granted Tyson a match that November. In the second round of the fight, Tyson caught Berbick with a powerful left hook, sending the champion to the canvas. He could not get up.

At twenty years old, Mike Tyson was the youngest heavyweight champion ever.

Tyson's next fight came in March 1987 against World Boxing Association (WBA) champion James "Bonecrusher" Smith. It proved to be Tyson's toughest fight to date. In the twelfth round, Smith caught Tyson with a punch right between the eyes. Tyson was dazed momentarily—then went after Smith, pummeling him repeatedly until the final bell. The decision was unanimous in Tyson's favor. Tyson had captured his second heavyweight title.

In May 1987, Tyson knocked out Pinklon Thomas in six rounds. Then, in August, Tyson beat Tony Tucker in a unanimous decision. It was Tyson's thirty-first victory without a defeat. In October, Tyson fought Tyrell Biggs. He knocked Biggs out in the seventh round.

By now, Tyson was considered unbeatable. There didn't seem to be any worthy opponents.

Former champion Larry Holmes was granted a match in January 1988, but he could not give Tyson much of a fight. Tyson knocked out Holmes in the fourth round.

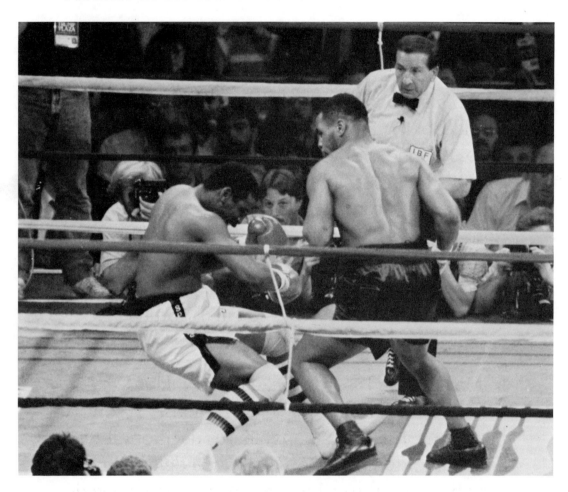

Mike Tyson knocks out Michael Spinks in ninety-one seconds.

In June 1988, Mike Tyson fought Michael Spinks for $21 million. The fight lasted ninety-one seconds as Tyson won in a knockout. Great Britain's Frank Bruno was Tyson's next opponent. Bruno lasted five rounds. In July 1989, Tyson fought Carl "The Truth" Williams. Williams was certain he would defeat Tyson, and boasted about it to the press. Tyson knocked out Williams after ninety-three seconds of the first round.

It seemed Mike Tyson would continue his amazing string of early knockouts forever. But then, in February 1990, the boxing world was stunned when Tyson was knocked out by Buster Douglas. Not only was it Tyson's first loss, it was the first time he had ever been knocked to the canvas.

Despite the loss, Mike Tyson has already established himself as one of boxing's greatest. His knockout record is one of the best, and few have rivaled his punching power. No doubt, Mike Tyson will be a boxing champion for many years to come.

The Brown Bomber

Joseph (Joe) Louis Barrow was born May 13, 1914, in Lafayette, Alabama. His father, Munroe, was a sharecropper. His grandfather had been a slave. Joe lived with his parents and six brothers and sisters in a shack on a cotton farm. It was a very hard life.

When Joe was twelve years old, he moved to Detroit, Michigan, with his mother, Lilly. There, Joe went to school for the first time. Since he could barely read or write, his teacher suggested that Joe be put into a vocational school where he could learn a trade. Joe learned to make furniture, then got a job in the nearby Ford Motor Company plant where he worked on the assembly line.

"The Brown Bomber" Joe Louis pictured here in June 1935.

25

One day, Joe walked into the Brewster Recreational Center in Detroit and saw his first boxing match. He took an instant liking to the sport, and soon found himself practicing his boxing skills. He grew into a strong young man. Louis stood 6 feet 1 inches tall and weighed 200 pounds. His quick and powerful left hook was his best punch.

In 1932, Joe fought his first amateur fight, using the name Joe Louis. Louis was knocked down seven times in just two rounds. But he got up each time, refusing to quit. By 1934, Louis was the best amateur fighter in Detroit. He had a record of 50-4 with 43 knockouts. And he had won the Amateur Athletic Union light heavyweight boxing championship. It was time to become a professional boxer.

On July 4, 1934, Joe Louis fought his first professional fight. He knocked out his opponent in the very first round. By June 1935, Louis had won 22 straight fights with 18 knockouts. The press began calling Louis "The Brown Bomber." His manager, John Roxborough, decided Louis was ready to contend for the heavyweight title. A match was set in New York against former heavyweight champion Primo Carnera. Louis knocked him out in the sixth round.

Louis beat another former champion, Max Baer, before losing his first fight to German heavyweight Max Schmeling in a 12-round knockout. Still, with a record of 34-1 with 29 knockouts, Louis was considered the top contender. The current champion, Jim Braddock, granted Louis a fight in 1937. Louis knocked Braddock out in the eighth round. Now, Joe Louis was heavyweight champion of the world.

Though he was on top, Louis still had a score to settle with Max Schmeling, the only professional fighter to beat Louis. A rematch was set for June 22, 1938. All of America sat glued to their radios as Louis fought Schmeling in front of 70,000 people at Yankee Stadium in New York. To most people, the fight represented America and freedom against Germany and the warlike Nazis, who were in power in Germany at the time.

Louis realized the importance of the fight from the very beginning. He immediately attacked Schmeling, swarming him with deadly punches.

Heavyweight Champion Joe Louis (right) and challenger Jersey Joe Walcott are tied up at close quarters during their 1948 fight.

After just two minutes and four seconds, the referee stopped the fight. Now Joe Louis was a hero to the world.

Joe Louis defended his title against Billy Conn in 1941 and barely won in a split decision. Then, when World War II broke out, Louis enlisted in the army, and did not return to boxing until 1946. He granted a rematch to Conn. This time, Louis had little trouble with Conn, knocking him out in the eighth round.

In 1947, Louis fought Jersey Joe Walcott. Louis was knocked down twice, but came back to win by a split decision. In 1948, a rematch was granted to Walcott. Louis was determined to do much better this time against his opponent, and he did, knocking out Walcott in the eleventh round. With no other goals to attain, Joe Louis decided to retire.

But his retirement was very short. Though Louis had made an incredible $4 million during his career, he had spent most of it. Even worse, he owed $250,000 in taxes. Since boxing was the only thing Joe Louis knew how to do, he was forced to return to the ring in 1950 to make more money. He fought the new heavyweight champion, Ezzard Charles, but lost in a unanimous decision.

Louis retired again, but in 1951, he came back to the ring in order to pay off more debts. Overweight and much slower, Louis won eight straight fights before his match with a young contender, Rocky Marciano. In the eighth round, Louis was sent to the canvas. The fight—and Louis's comeback attempt—was over. Louis retired for good after the fight.

Joe Louis went on to work in Las Vegas as a host in a casino where he worked many, many years to pay off his debts. In 1981, Joe Louis died. But his legacy as one of the greatest boxers of all-time lives on. Joe Louis's twelve-year reign as heavyweight champion of the world (1937-49) is still a record. So too are his twenty-five successful title defenses. Because boxing is such a physically punishing sport, it is unlikely these records will ever be broken.

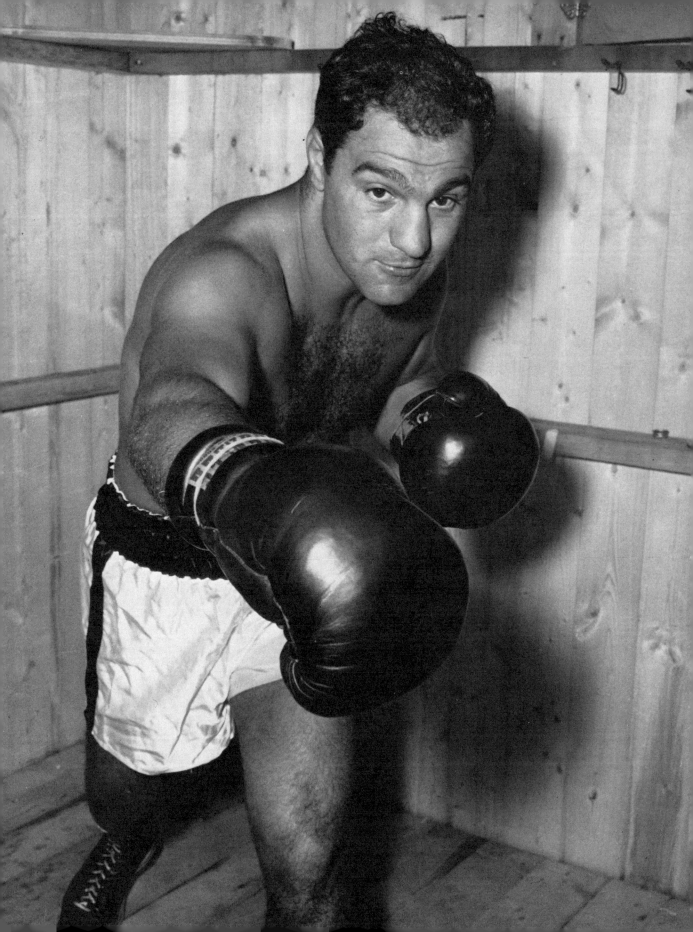

Rocky

Rocco Francis Marchegiano (Rocky Marciano) was born September 1, 1923, in Brockton, Massachusetts. His father, an Italian immigrant, was a shoemaker. The Marcianos were very poor, and when Rocky was fourteen years old, he had to quit school to help support his family. Rocky worked a variety of jobs, including candy-making, ditch digging, and truck driving. When he had free time, Marciano liked to play football and baseball.

Rocky Marciano

Marciano did not think about boxing until he was in an army camp in Wales, England, during World War II. Because he was known to be tough and strong, Marciano was asked by his friends to fight a camp bully. Marciano agreed and fought the bully in a makeshift boxing ring. Marciano knocked out the bully in the second round.

Marciano was sent to Fort Lewis in Washington where he fought as an amateur. After his discharge in 1946, Marciano decided to pursue a baseball career. He tried out for the Chicago Cubs as a catcher. But Marciano was cut because of his poor throwing. With nowhere else to go, Marciano turned to amateur boxing.

Marciano won all his amateur boxing matches before losing in the amateur championship fight. But afterwards, Marciano was convinced he could become a professional fighter.

His first professional fight came on March 17, 1947. He knocked out his opponent in three rounds. Marciano stood 5 feet 11 inches and weighed only 185 pounds. His reach was short for a boxer (68 inches compared to Joe Louis's 76-inch reach), but his punches were extremely powerful. Marciano's power caught the eye of boxing manager Al Weill, who signed Marciano. In his first fight for Weill (July 19, 1948), Marciano knocked out his opponent in the third round. Marciano finished the year with 11 knockouts in 11 fights.

In 1949, Marciano had another great year. He fought 13 fights with 11 knockouts. But after his fight on December 30, Marciano nearly quit boxing. He had just sent his opponent, Carmine Vingo, to the hospital with a severe concussion. Marciano vowed to quit boxing if Vingo died. Vingo survived, but remained paralyzed from the waist down. Marciano paid $2,000 towards Vingo's medical expenses, and won the hearts of boxing fans everywhere.

Despite Marciano's fine year, Al Weill was concerned. For the first time in his short career, Marciano had failed to knock out an opponent. Weill wondered if Marciano could survive a long boxing match with a clever fighter. The following year, Marciano answered his manager by winning a decision over a tough opponent named LaStarza. Now Marciano was ready to make a run at the heavyweight title.

Rocky Marciano (left) knocks down the British champion, Don Cockell, for the second time in round number 9. Cockell rose to his feet, but staggered until the referee stopped the fight.

In 1951, Marciano fought the legendary Joe Louis. By then, Louis's career was nearly over, and he was attempting a final comeback. Marciano had little difficulty knocking out Louis in eight rounds. Afterwards, Marciano felt so bad about ending Louis's career, he sent a letter of apology to Louis.

On July 28, 1952, Marciano fought his first real heavyweight contender, Harry "Kid" Matthews. Marciano used his powerful right hook—a punch he would become famous for—to knock out Matthews in the second round. Suddenly, Rocky Marciano was considered a heavyweight contender, and he was granted a title match with the current champion, Jersey Joe Walcott.

The title match was staged on September 23, 1952, in Philadelphia's Municipal Stadium. In the first round, Marciano was stunned by a left hook and—for the first time in his career—was knocked to the canvas. Marciano got up immediately and stalked Jersey Joe Walcott relentlessly.

Marciano took a lot of punches. He had a cut above his right eye which made it difficult for him to see. But Marciano delivered just as many punches to Walcott. Finally, in the thirteenth round, Marciano wore out Walcott with his relentless punching and knocked him out. Suddenly, Rocky Marciano was the heavyweight champion of the world. He started to jump and holler with joy—until he saw his crumpled opponent. Marciano halted his celebration, realizing how badly Walcott was feeling about losing.

Eight months later, Marciano gave Walcott a rematch. Again, Marciano punched his opponent relentlessly. This time, Marciano knocked out Walcott after two minutes of the first round.

Marciano defended his title five more times. He knocked out Roland LaStarza in 11 rounds. Then Marciano experienced his toughest title defense when he went the distance with Ezzard Charles. After a bloody battle, Marciano outpointed Charles and kept his heavyweight title. Charles was given a rematch, and this time Marciano swarmed Charles with devastating punches. Charles managed one strong punch to Marciano's face. Marciano just blinked, then finished off Charles with a powerful right hook.

Charles landed on the canvas face-first, and the fight was over.

Don Cockell, the British Champion, was the next victim. Marciano knocked him out in 9 rounds. Marciano's final fight was against Archie Moore. Moore knocked Marciano down in the first round But Marciano quickly sprung to his feet and pounded his opponent relentlessly. By the ninth round, Moore was bloody and battered. A powerful right hook by Marciano buckled Moore's knees, and then he slumped to the canvas. Marciano had won his last fight by a knockout.

On April 27, 1956, Rocky Marciano announced his retirement. He was married and had a child, and wanted to spend more time with them. Besides, he had earned an incredible $4 million — a lot of money in those days.

Tragically, Rocky Marciano died in a plane crash in Iowa on August 31, 1969, at the age of forty-six. Still, Rocky Marciano remains one of the all-time great boxers. In his 49 professional fights, Marciano won by knockout 43 times. Even greater, Marciano was the first and only *undefeated* heavyweight champion of the world.

The Greatest

Cassius Clay was born January 17, 1942, in Louisville, Kentucky. His father was a house painter. His grandfather had been a slave. Life was tough for young Cassius. His family was always poor. Cassius learned to fight on the playgrounds of Louisville, first with rocks, then with his fists.

His ability to fight led Clay to neighborhood gymnasiums where he discovered the sport of boxing. Clay spent many hours in the gyms and practiced his boxing technique. When he became old enough, Clay entered the amateur ranks,

Muhammed Ali

fighting in Golden Glove tournaments. By the time he was eighteen years old, Clay had won 108 fights with eight defeats. Six times he had won the Kentucky Gold Gloves, and twice he won the National Amateur Athletic Union championships.

In 1960, Clay was selected to represent the United States in the Olympics in Rome, Italy. He fought as a light heavyweight, and knocked out four consecutive opponents to win the gold medal.

When he returned to Louisville, Clay received many offers from professional boxing promoters. He signed with Billy Reynolds, a wealthy businessman, for $10,000 plus $500 each month. Clay would have to split his earnings evenly with Reynolds.

Clay was six feet tall, weighed two hundred pounds, had extremely fast hands and a very long reach. He could dance around his opponents and jab at them mercilessly while they struggled to keep up with him. His fights usually ended with a knockout.

Clay won his first six professional fights—usually by the fourth round. Only one fight was won by decision. Clay's confidence grew with each knockout, and he began predicting before each fight the round in which his opponent would fall. Typically, his predictions came in the form of poetry. Before his fight with veteran Archie Moore, Clay said:

"Archie's been living off the fat of the land,

I'm here to give him his pension plan,

When you come to the fight, don't block the door,

You will go home after round four."

Clay knocked Moore out in the fourth round.

Clay continued to win. By 1963, he was undefeated as a professional boxer, and was given a shot at the heavyweight title against Sonny Liston. Everyone thought Liston would win. But Clay used his long reach to pound the heavyweight champ. "Float like a butterfly, sting like a bee!" Clay's trainers shouted during the fight. By the end of the seventh round, Liston had injured his shoulder and could not fight. Clay was declared the new heavyweight champion.

Afterwards, Clay told the world he was a Black Muslim, and that he wanted to be called Muhammed Ali.

Ali defended his title ferociously. In his first fight as champ in 1965, he knocked out Sonny Liston in the first round. He then went on to win a string of eight fights until he got into trouble with the government in 1967.

Ali had been drafted. But since he was a Black Muslim, he refused to enter the army. His religion forbid him to fight in the Vietnam War. Ali was convicted of draft evasion. He was fined $10,000, stripped of his heavyweight title, and was barred from professional boxing.

Ali did not return to boxing until 1970 after the Supreme Court ruled he could not be banned from boxing. Ali fought Oscar Bonavena, and won in a fifteen-round knockout. "I'm the greatest!" Ali shouted after the fight. Now he was ready to take a shot at the current heavyweight champion, Joe Frazier.

Ali predicted he would knockout Frazier in six. But Ali was not the boxer he was when he was known as Cassius Clay. The powerful Joe Frazier was at the height of his career, and he pummeled Ali throughout the match. In the final round, Frazier knocked Ali to the canvas. Ali got up and finished the fight, but Frazier won by unanimous decision, and remained heavyweight champion.

Ali wanted a rematch. But before it could be arranged, Frazier fought George Foreman in 1973 and lost. Now Foreman was champion. During that time, Ali decided to fight Ken Norton. Norton surprised Ali—and the world—by winning the fight by decision. Afterwards it was discovered that Norton had broken Ali's jaw in the first round.

To get a shot at the title, Ali first had to defeat Norton. A rematch was set for September 1973. Ali won in a close decision. But before he got a shot at Foreman, Ali had to beat Joe Frazier.

Ali trained hard for the fight and weighed in at 212 pounds. Ali stunned Frazier early in the match, and Frazier could never recover. Ali won unanimously. Now it was on to a title fight with George Foreman.

Foreman would be a difficult foe. He was taller and stronger than Ali, and Ali had to be clever if he wanted to become champion again.

*Champion Sonny Liston grimaces as Cassius Clay
shakes him up with a left in the sixth round. Clay
upset Liston by beating him in the seventh round.*

On March 26, 1974, Ali fought Foreman in Caracas, Venezuela. But instead of attacking Foreman, Ali stood along the ropes and let Foreman hit him at will. Foreman could never deliver a knockout blow, and started growing tired. That's when Ali came after Foreman. In the eighth round, Ali dropped Foreman to the canvas. The fight was over. Ali's strategy against Foreman became known as "rope-a-dope." Ali was heavyweight champion for the second time.

Ali defended his title against Chuck Wepner in 1975. Ali was knocked to the canvas for only the fourth time in his career, and beat Wepner in a last round knockout. Two victories later, Ali granted Joe Frazier a rematch. It became known as the "Thrilla in Manila" because it was held in the Philippines. Ali took the early rounds, but Frazier fought back hard and took control of the match. But just as it seemed Ali would lose, he hammered Frazier in the fourteenth round. Frazier could not finish the fight, and Ali retained his title.

In February 1978, Ali faced Olympic champion Leon Spinks. No one gave Spinks a chance, but he surprized everyone by beating Ali in a unanimous decision. Ali was granted a rematch in September, and this time he was ready for Spinks. Ali won the decision—and became the first fighter to ever win the heavyweight title three different times.

Ali announced his retirement shortly after, but came back to fight former sparring partner Larry Holmes in 1980. Ali was thirty-eight years old, and no match for the younger and stronger Holmes. The fight was stopped in the tenth round, and afterwards, Ali announced his retirement again.

But Ali was lured from that short retirement one more time to fight Trevor Berbick in December 1981. Now nearing forty, Ali lasted the entire ten-round match. Still, he was no longer the boxer he used to be, and he lost by decision. The following day, December 12, 1981, Muhammed Ali announced his official retirement.

In 21 years of professional boxing, Muhammed Ali amassed a record of 56-5 while earning a record $69 million. Single-handedly, he made heavyweight boxing the spectacular and popular sporting event that it is today. No doubt, Muhammed Ali was "The Greatest."